Dale Earnhardt Jr.

RACE CAR DRIVER

Josepha Sherman

P.O. Box 196
Hockessin, Delaware 19707
Visit us on the web: www.mitchelllane.com
Comments? email us: mitchelllane@mitchelllane.com

NL

Printing   2   3   4   5   6   7   8   9

A Robbie Reader

Library of Congress Cataloging-in-Publication Data
Sherman, Josepha.
    Dale Earnhardt Jr. / by Josepha Sherman.
        p. cm. – (A robbie reader)
    Includes bibliographical references and index.
    ISBN 1-58415-360-1 (library bound)
    1. Earnhardt, Dale, Jr. — Juvenile literature. 2. Automobile racing drivers — United States — Biography — Juvenile literature. I. Title. II. Series.
GV1032.E19S44 2005
796.72'092 — dc22
                                                                                    2004030742
ISBN-10: 1-58415-360-1   ISBN-13: 978-1-58415-360-3

ABOUT THE AUTHOR: Josepha Sherman is a prolific author with more than 60 books in print. The owner of Sherman Editorial Services, she has also written a six-book series on alternative energy (Capstone); *The History of the Internet* (Franklin Watts); *Bill Gates: Computer King* (Millbrook); and *Syd Hoff, The Story of Harley-Davidson, Johnny Gruelle and the Story of Raggedy Ann and Andy,* and *Dale Earnhardt Jr.* for Mitchell Lane Publishers. She is a native New Yorker, has a degree in archaeology, loves to tinker with computers, and follows the NY Mets.

PHOTO CREDITS: Cover, pp. 4, 7, 16, 20 (top), 22, 25, 26 — Sean Doughtery; p. 8 — David Taylor/Allsport; p. 10 (top) — Terry Renna, Stringer/Associated Press; p. 10 (bottom) — Harold Hinson, Stringer/Associated Press; pp. 12, 24, 28 — Kevin Kane/ WireImage; p. 15 — Dale Atkins/Associated Press; p. 18 (top) — Stringer/Associated Press; p. 18 (bottom) — Bill Stafford/Associated Press; p. 21 (bottom) — Jamie Squire/ Getty Images.

ACKNOWLEDGMENTS: The following story has been thoroughly researched, and to the best of our knowledge, represents a true story. While every possible effort has been made to ensure accuracy, the publisher will not assume liability for damages caused by inaccuracies in the data, and makes no warranty on the accuracy of the information contained herein. This story has not been authorized or endorsed by Dale Earnhardt Jr. or anyone associated with Dale Earnhardt Jr.

PCG2-24-28-29-32

TABLE OF CONTENTS

Dale Earnhardt Jr. takes driving a race car very seriously, and he enjoys life as well. He hopes to keep racing and winning for many years to come.

A Rookie at the Daytona 500

The stands at the Daytona, Florida, racetrack were crowded in 2000. People were talking and cheering. The Daytona 500 was about to start. It was one of the most famous car races in America. It was the first race of the **Winston Cup**.

The track was a big oval. It was two and a half miles around. Its outer edge was higher than its inner edge. Drivers had to race two hundred **laps**, or complete circles, around the track. Two hundred **laps** would equal five hundred miles. Whoever finished first would be the winner.

It was Dale Earnhardt Jr.'s first Daytona 500. He was a rookie, a new driver. He had never even seen the race in person.

5

Dale climbed into his car and strapped himself in. The safety harness had five belts to hold him in the driver's seat. It also had a quick-release latch in case he had to get out in a hurry. Next he put on dark goggles to protect his eyes, and a safety helmet painted with his team number, 8.

He heard the words that begin every car race: *"Gentlemen, start your engines!"*

The race starter's green flag dropped. They were off!

Dale was surrounded by other cars. Every driver was trying to find the best position. Dale had to get a good position. He also had to keep from crashing into any other cars. The cars were all going very fast. There wasn't much time to think. But Dale, like the other drivers, had a race **spotter**. The **spotter** could see the whole race. He helped Dale move through traffic.

On **lap** number 156, all the cars were ordered to make a **pit stop**. The **pit** is a space on the inside of the track, where the driver's

mechanics are ready to work on their cars. They work very fast. They replace worn tires, fill the fuel tank, and do any other repairs that the car needs. They do all that in about 18 seconds. Dale's team replaced two of his tires.

All the cars left the **pit stop**. Dale found himself in second place. Could he win? Suddenly the more experienced drivers passed him. Dale finished thirteenth, but at least he was no longer a rookie. He knew that one day he would win the Daytona 500.

Dale's pit crew works on his car, changing tires, filling the gas tank, and making any other repairs. The crew moves quickly so that Dale can get back on the track in a good position. A pit crew can help their driver win or lose a race.

7

Dale raced in the Busch series of car racing before he went on to drive in the Winston Cup (now Nextel Cup). In his career as a Busch Series driver, Dale has won two championships, one in 1998 and one in 1999. Is he thinking of winning another race in this picture?

Dale's Early Days

Ralph Dale Earnhardt Jr. was born on October 10, 1974, in Concord, North Carolina, near the family's home in Mooresville. His parents were **NASCAR** star Dale Earnhardt and Brenda Gee. She was the daughter of Robert Gee, a well-known **NASCAR mechanic**. Their marriage broke up after the births of Dale and his sister, Kelley. Dale was raised by his father and Teresa Earnhardt, Dale's stepmother.

Dale grew up around race cars and racetracks. Successful race car drivers had big houses in Mooresville. The town was full of car racing stores. Mooresville has been nicknamed Race City USA.

Teresa Earnhardt loves her stepson. She made sure that Dale went to school. Those

Dale Jr. with his stepmother, Teresa Earnhardt. Teresa loves her stepson. Together, they run Dale Earnhardt Incorporated.

Dale's sister, Kelley. She raced as a teenager, but Kelley left racing to go to college.

days weren't easy for him. He was a small, shy boy. He stood only five and a half feet tall until after high school. Then Dale suddenly grew to be six feet tall.

Dale's grandfather, Ralph Earnhardt, had been a professional **NASCAR** driver. He was on the top fifty list of **NASCAR** drivers. Dale's father was also a top racing driver. He was called the Intimidator. That means someone who scares other people. He was called that because he drove without fear. He thought that Dale should try racing, too. Children under the age of thirteen can race in go-karts. A go-kart is a small, low car with a small engine.

Dale and his kart didn't seem to like each other. He says, "Most of the time I was being run over or thrown off my own kart."

His father saw this. He told Dale to wait a few years before he tried to become a racer.

11

Dale Jr. poses in front of his 2005 Busch Series car in Daytona. His car number is 81, and his sponsor is Nabisco. Car numbers, sponsors, and paint schemes on cars often change in Nascar.

The Professional Driver

Dale has a half brother, Kerry. Dale, Kerry, and their sister Kelley all wanted to be race car drivers. When they were teenagers, they put their money together. They bought a car with it. It was an old Monte Carlo. They raced it on short tracks, teaching themselves how to race. They didn't win very often, but Dale says, "We certainly learned a lot—especially about how to repair crash damage."

Kelley soon left to go to college. She didn't return to racing. Dale went to Mitchell Community College for an **automotive diploma**. The school would teach him how to work on cars. He drove his car at races whenever he could. He did all the repair work himself. He still wasn't winning too much, but

13

Dale was having fun. He was getting better and better at race car driving.

In 1998, Dale won his first series of races, the Busch Series. It is run on several tracks. He won the same series in 1999. Dale was now a professional.

His father and stepmother had given their **racing team** a new name. It was called Dale Earnhardt Incorporated, or DEI. Dale Sr. knew that his son was a good race car driver. In 2000, he brought Dale into his team. Dale would race in the **Winston Cup**. Now officially called the **Nextel Cup**, it is **NASCAR**'s most important series of races. The thirty-six races in the series are held at tracks all across the United States. The driver who wins the most races and earns the most points wins the Cup. Dale's father had won the championship seven times.

NASCAR fans like to pick one driver to follow. Many of them picked Dale Earnhardt Jr. They wanted to see how the son would do against his famous father.

It took Dale twelve tries. Finally, in 2000, he had his first **Winston Cup** win in Fort Worth, Texas. He got his second win four races later in Richmond, Virginia. After that, he began to win more often. By the end of 2000, he had earned over $2 million in prize money. People said Dale was one of the best new drivers in **NASCAR**.

Dale Jr. (left) with his father, Dale Sr. (center), and his half brother Kerry (right). All three men are race car drivers. Now, after Dale Sr.'s death, his sons still race on—Dale Jr. in the Nextel Cup Series, and Kerry in the Craftsman Truck Series.

Dale Earnhardt Sr., also known as "The Intimidator," spent most of his life as a race car driver. He won seven Winston Cup Championships and finally had his one and only Daytona 500 win in the year 2000. He died the next year in a crash on the last lap of the Daytona 500.

Tragedy and Triumph

The 2001 Daytona 500 looked as if it would be a good race for both Dale Sr. and Dale Jr. Everyone picked Dale Sr. to win. During the race, his car, number 3, was hit by another car. Number 3 went out of control. It smashed into a wall. Dale Earnhardt Sr. was killed.

Everyone who followed **NASCAR** was shocked. It didn't seem possible that Dale Sr. was dead.

Dale Jr. was amazed to learn how many people had loved his father. Strangers wrote letters, painted pictures, and wrote poems about Dale Sr. It was comforting to Dale and the rest of the Earnhardt family. Dale said, "It makes me feel good to see what he meant to so many people."

The top portion of this photo is the wreck that Dale Jr. had one week after his father's wreck (shown below it). Unfortunately, his father was killed instantly in the crash.

Dale Jr. barely escapes serious injury during a practice session for the American Le Mans Series in July 2004.

Dale was very sad, but he knew that his father would have wanted him to keep racing. One week after his father's death, Dale took part in a race. But he crashed into a wall—just as his father had done. The crowds held their breath. To their great relief, Dale Jr. was only bruised and shaken up. He knew that he would keep on racing.

The death of Dale Sr. was not the only tragedy in 2001. On September 11, 2001, there were terrorist attacks on the United States. Thousands of U.S. citizens were killed. The world grieved. Most **professional** sporting events were delayed, including the race at Dover Downs International Speedway in Dover, Delaware. The race was held two weeks after the attack, on September 23. People feared another attack on U.S. citizens, so security at every major sporting event was at its highest. But fear did not stop the true race fans from showing up at Dover Downs that day to watch Dale Jr. win the race. The crowds cried tears of sadness and tears of joy as Dale drove around the track displaying the American flag with honor and pride.

19

Racing fans loved Dale Earnhardt Sr. They were stunned when he died. Fans left a collection of photos, clothing, pictures, and poetry to the Earnhardt family.

On September 11, 2001, terrorists attacked the United States. Two weeks later, the Dover Downs Cal Ripken Jr. 400 was held, even though people were still worried about other attacks. Dale Jr. won the race.

In racing, crashes are common. Unfortunately, they are sometimes fatal. **NASCAR** has come a long way to make sure the drivers have the best safety equipment to keep them from serious injury.

Like many drivers, Dale will sometimes race in other car series. On July 18, 2004, Dale was driving a Corvette C5-R at a practice session for the American Le Mans Series in Sonoma, California. His car spun out and caught fire. Dale made it out of the car alive, but not without burns on his face and neck. After the wreck, Dale immediately thought of his father. He was heard to say that it was his father who had pulled him from the burning car. Dale Sr.

may not have really pulled him from the car, but many people believe that he was looking down on his son that day, watching over him.

Dale proudly holds his trophy for winning his first Daytona 500. Will there be more Daytona wins for Dale? Only time will tell.

On to the Future

In 2003, Dale had so many wins that he was voted **NASCAR**'s Most Popular Driver. He earned about $9 million that year.

In 2004, Dale's dream finally came true. He won the Daytona 500. He didn't stop there, though. Dale continued to race, and to win, throughout the year.

As long as Dale stays healthy and without serious injury, he says he will keep on racing, and his **racing team** will stay with him. Tony Eury Sr., the head of the team, was named Crew Chief of the Year in 2004.

Dale will also continue to race in the **NASCAR** Busch Series when he can, as long as it doesn't interfere with his chances of progressing in the **Nextel Cup** series. If Dale isn't driving in the Busch Series, you might see him cheering on his driver Martin Truex Jr.

Companies sponsor **NASCAR**. They pay to have their ads on the race cars, the drivers' clothing, and the racetracks. They want the drivers to endorse their products. This means that the driver will say how much he or she likes the product, such as a shoe or a drink. Dale is surprised to see how many companies want to sponsor him. He won't endorse shoes

Dale is the car owner for Busch series driver Martin Truex Jr. (left). Martin won the Busch series championship in 2004 and 2005.

because, he says, "I like being able to wear whatever shoes I want to wear." And he adds, "Hey, this is me, and I'm not going to dress differently for you." He does endorse Nabisco, because he likes their cookies!

Dale still lives in Mooresville, North Carolina. He and his stepmother, Teresa, run the business that his father started. It is still called Dale Earnhardt Incorporated. By now, it takes up space in a big collection of buildings. There is a race shop, an office building, a museum, and even a souvenir store.

In NASCAR, drivers have many sponsors. In the Busch Series, Dale drove this number 3 Oreo car, sponsored by Nabisco. He won the Daytona 300 in this car.

When Dale isn't racing, he likes to live like an ordinary person. He's glad that people don't stop him on the street to ask for autographs. Dale says that off the racetrack, he doesn't want to be recognized. He loves to party with his friends, surf the Internet, and play computer games. He and his sister Kelley keep up his Web site. Dale roots for the Washington Redskins football team. He even likes to go to the local mall and just hang out.

Like his father, Dale is active in charities, such as The Dale Earnhardt Foundation,

After winning his first Daytona 500, Dale Jr. scrambles happily out of his car. He's grinning from ear to ear. Who can blame him for being happy?

Speedway Children's Charities, and the Victory Junction Gang, which benefits children with chronic and life threatening illnesses.

Dale has recently teamed up with Polaris Industries to make a program to help the Victory Junction Gang Camp. Polaris Industries makes recreational (rek-ree-AY-shuh-nul) vehicles like ATVs (all-terrain vehicles). Polaris will help pay for kids to go to the Victory Junction Gang Camp depending on how well Dale races every week. Each time Dale finishes in the top 8, Polaris will pay for a week-long stay for one camper.

Along with Dale's caring side, he is a champion **NASCAR** driver. He is also just a plain "nice guy."

The crew chief is the most important member of the pit crew. Tony Eury Sr. was honored in 2004 as Crew Chief of the Year. Here, Tony and Dale are probably discussing their strategy. In 2005, Tony Eury Jr. took over as Dale's crew chief.

1974   Ralph Dale Earnhardt Jr. is born on October 10.

1998   Dale wins his first professional racing series, the Busch Series.

1999   Dale wins the Busch Series again.

2000   Dale becomes a professional race car driver with his father's team; finishes 16th in the points.

2001   Dale Earnhardt Sr. dies in a racing accident; Dale Jr. finishes 8th in the points

2002   Dale's book, *Driver #8,* becomes a bestseller; finishes 11th in the points

2003   Dale is voted NASCAR's Most Popular Driver; finishes 3rd in the points

2004   Dale wins the Daytona 500; finishes 5th in the points.

2005   Polaris teams up with Dale Jr. to benefit the Victory Junction Gang Camp; Dale Jr. and Orange 21 announce the launch of Dale Earnhardt Jr. signature sunglasses series "E Eyewear"; according to a Harris Poll, Dale Jr. is ranked 8th as the most favorite sports star; Dale finishes 19th in the Nextel Cup; he won his third straight Chex Most Popular Driver.

TO FIND OUT MORE

For Young Readers

Kelly, K.C. *NASCAR: Racing to the Finish.* Pleasantville, New York: Readers Digest Press, 2005.

Kirkpatrick, Rob. *Dale Earnhardt Jr.: NASCAR Road Racer.* New York: Rosen Publishing, 2001.

Stewart, Mark. *Dale Earnhardt, Jr.: Driven by Destiny.* Milford, Connecticut: Millbrook Press, 2003.

On the Internet

The Official Site of Dale Earnhardt Jr.
www.dalejr.com

The Official NASCAR Site
www.nascar.com

All About Dale
www.dalejrpitstop.com

Dale Fans
www.dalejr.net

Dale Earnhardt Information
www.daleearnhardt.net

Dale Earnhardt News
www.daleearnhardtinc.com

automotive diploma (AW-toe-moe-tiv DIH-ploh-mah)—a college certificate earned after two years of studying all about cars.

lap—in racing, a complete circling of the track.

mechanic (mih-KAN-ik)—a person who works on a car to keep it running.

NASCAR—the National Association of Stock Car Automobile Racing, the organization that sponsors most stock car racing.

pit—the area at the side of a racetrack where a car is repaired or refueled during a race; there is one pit for each racing team.

pit crew—the mechanics of a racing team who work in the pit.

pit stop—a stop during a car race for maintenance work.

professional (pro-FEH-shuh-nul)—a person who is paid to perform.

racing team—all the people, as many as forty, for one car or series of cars; the team includes the owner, the driver, the spotter, mechanics, and others.

spotter—the person who watches for clear driving room or problems on the track and radios them to the driver during a race.

stock car—a car built for stock car racing, heavier than the cars used in regular car racing but faster than ordinary automobiles.

Winston Cup—since 1972, the most important series of NASCAR races, which begins with the Daytona 500 in February of every year. In 2004, the name was changed to the Nextel Cup.